WITHDRAWN

D0897733

Short Story Writers and Their Work

A GUIDE TO THE BEST

Brad Hooper

American Library Association • Chicago and London 1988

Designed by Harriett Banner

Composed by Precision Typographers
on a Quadex/Compugraphic 8400
system in Sabon and Bodoni Book

Printed on 50-pound Glatfelter, a
pH-neutral stock, and bound in
65-pound Nekoosa cover stock by
Malloy Lithographing, Inc.

The paper used in this publication meets the minimum requirements of American National Standard for Information Sciences—Permanence of Paper for Printed Library Materials, ANSI Z39.48-1984.

Library of Congress Cataloging-in-Publication Data

Hooper, Brad.
  Short story writers and their work.

  Includes index.
  1. Short story.   2. Short stories—Stories, plots,
etc.   3. Bibliography—Best books—Short stories.
I. Title.
PN3373.H6 1988   809.3′1   88-10393
ISBN 0-8389-0485-8

For Jim

I am grateful to Martin Brady
for the exceptional conscientiousness
with which he wielded his blue pencil.

Contents

Introduction

In the 1980s, the short story in the United States experienced a renaissance, generating a greater publishing and readership interest than in previous decades. Not only was the short story attracting a growing number of new writers, but it also succeeded in maintaining within its boundaries all the well-established practitioners of the form.

Editors of annual anthologies of superior short stories have commented on this situation. Even more frequently, book critics point it out in newspaper and magazine reviews of short-story collections. The renaissance is being called a celebration: the short-story anthology is no longer the Cinderella who must stay home from the publishing ball. While it might not be the fair maiden who catches the prince's eye (*that* is usually the blockbuster novel), the collection of stories is still allowed to partake of the festivities (big press runs, lots of publicity, receipt of literary prizes).

It is also true that extremely talented fiction writers are not simply churning out short stories during the idle hours in-between novels. Instead, they focus as much of their talent on the writing of short fiction as they do on their novels—in some cases, more so.

Just what are the reasons for this new solid state of the genre? No one seems to know for certain, but the critical literature and short-story anthologies offer ample discussion of this question.

Suggested answers center on two points. One, that in this highly technological, fast-paced society, the short story is perfectly suited to the limited fragments of reading time available in our busy days. Two, that the mushrooming graduate-level university writing programs throughout the country have produced writers, who, on a regular basis, are capable of filling mailboxes to the brim with envelopes containing quite publishable material.

A lot of credit should go to the editors of the proliferating literary quarterlies in the United States—for choosing the best, as they see it, from this growing pile of manuscripts; for always seeking to discover new talent while supporting the careers of already recognized story writers.

How do current story writers themselves feel about this renaissance? Andre Dubus, a major figure among the younger generation of authors performing brilliantly these days, perhaps spoke for most of his peers when he said in an interview, "I think that short stories have a great future. There used to be more magazines to publish them. But who can say there's no place to publish stories today? True, you won't get rich, but I'm convinced, too, that book publishers today are realizing that short stories are not necessarily a losing proposition."[1]

Just what *is* a short story?

Most people would answer that it is a piece of fiction much shorter than a novel.

While that response is true, it is more than just length that separates the short story from the novel.

Edgar Allan Poe was an important American story writer. In a review of Nathaniel Hawthorne's story collection, *Twice-Told Tales* (published in 1837), Poe issued what has become a classic position paper on the definition of a short story:

> As the novel cannot be read at one sitting, it cannot avail itself of the immense benefit of *totality*. Worldly interests, intervening during the pauses of perusal, modify, counteract, and annul the impressions intended. But simply cessation in reading would, of itself, be sufficient to destroy the true unity. In the brief tale, however, the author is enabled to carry out his full design without interruption. During the hours of perusal, the soul of the reader is at the writer's control.
>
> A skilful artist has constructed a tale. He has not fashioned his thoughts to accommodate his incidents, but having deliberately conceived a certain *single effect* to be wrought, he then invents such incidents, he then combines such events, and discusses them in such a tone as may best serve him in establishing this preconceived effect. If his very first sentence tend not to the out-bringing of this effect, then in his very first step has he committed a blunder. In the whole composition there should be no word written of which the tendency, direct or indirect, is not to the one pre-established design. And by such means, with such

care and skill, a picture is at length painted which leaves in the mind of him who contemplates it with a kindred art, a sense of the fullest satisfaction. The idea of the tale, its thesis, has been presented unblemished, because undisturbed—an end absolutely demanded, yet, in the novel, altogether unattainable.[2]

That is the best definition, I feel, of the short story—different from a novel in that it is short enough to be read in one sitting, with *every* word leading toward some final, pre-ordained effect.

Suppose a writer wanted to write a short story about a marriage—a long marriage of, say, fifty years. The writer would not tell the whole history of that marriage, even if he were to condense the main events into twenty pages. By doing that, he'd simply be writing a condensed novel. No, a short story about such a marriage would isolate one moment—a dialogue over a meal, a weekend together, an interaction with other couples at a party, an encounter with children or grandchildren—that reveals the whole state of their relationship.

It's not an easy task; successful short stories are harder to write than it may initially appear.

This guide to the short story emphasizes writers over individual works—although within each discussion, I cite an exemplary story or two or three. Isolating the particular stories or editions or compilations cited here is less important than bringing to your attention the writers themselves. In most instances, the collection listed under each author is only a sample of what is in print. Let the books listed serve as a starting point. It is up to you, if you so desire, to seek more collections upon discovering a writer you especially like. Familiarity with these men and women will make you conversant in the short story indeed.

1. "PW Interviews," *Publishers Weekly* 226:56–57 (Oct. 12, 1984).
2. *The Story and Its Writer: An Introduction to Short Fiction.* Ann Charters, ed. St. Martin's, 1983, paper (0-312-76251-8). p.1123–24.

The Masters of the Past

The short story seems a logical form of expression. You can easily imagine cave people sitting around a fire, relating made-up events to entertain themselves. To have the complete narrative done within a few minutes—and a new one every night—would certainly be more satisfying to an audience than dragging out a long narrative over several evenings. Otherwise, the teller would run the risk of losing the listeners' interest.

Into recorded history, short fictitious narratives flourished as mythical tales, passing on cultural identities or providing sheer entertainment. But it was not until the nineteenth century that the short story as we know it was recognized as a distinct literary genre. It became an art form, with rules. Edgar Allan Poe's definition, cited previously, was part of this movement—including writers here in the United States and abroad (particularly in France, Germany, and Russia)—to produce stories according to certain guidelines for structure and technique. These guidelines centered on the premise that the short fictional narrative is best suited to the purpose of delivering a glancing blow, a vital glimpse of character.

The men and women who follow, none still living, are the masters who either contributed to the birth of the short story in the nineteenth century (in what we perceive as its "modern" garb) or were in the forefront of making it an even more integral literary form in the twentieth century. These are the writers whom I feel still retain the most appeal to contemporary readers, who are most relevant to anyone wanting to experience the artistic integrity of this literary form.

SHERWOOD ANDERSON
American. 1876–1941.

Legend has it that one day, in 1912, Anderson simply picked up and walked out of his Ohio paint factory to devote himself to writing. Whether it happened exactly that way or not, he produced in 1919 a classic in *Winesburg, Ohio,* a cycle of interrelated stories that viewed, sympathetically, lonely, frustrated individuals in a fictitious midwestern town. Anderson's direct style influenced a generation of U.S. fiction writers, Hemingway and Faulkner among them; however, some readers may now find his writing occasionally simplistic and even unrefined. Nonetheless, Anderson could drive quickly, seemingly effortlessly, to the core of the Winesburgers' distress. *Winesburg* can be read straight through as a novel; or, just a few of the component tales can be delved into and fully appreciated individually. The story "Hands" is both exemplary and the most affecting of those in the collection. It concerns a man who must keep hidden his fluttery hands, which once, because of their excessive expressiveness, got him into dire trouble.

Anderson, Sherwood. *Winesburg, Ohio.* 247p. Penguin, paper, $3.95 (0-14-039059-6).

H. E. BATES
English. 1905–74.

Bates reached great heights in his critical and popular reputations in the 1930s, when the short story in Britain was enjoying a revival. He was from Northamptonshire—a rural environment. His tales are derived from the land, his characters earthy and sensuous—the colors and smells and even the warmth or chilly breezes of the countryside all pervade his stunning stories. Bates wrote with fine and moving lyricism, his sentences fraught with calm beauty. He often probed the steaminess that exists when a man and a woman, both secretly boiling with passion, find themselves in close proximity, or the very human foibles of charming rustic characters. His *Uncle Silas* sequence is sheer delight: humorous, poignant, positively endearing—and with a vivid delineation of the title character.

Bates, H. E. *The Best of H. E. Bates.* Ayer, $24.50 (0-8369-3967-0).

Bates, H. E. *My Uncle Silas.* Oxford, paper, $5.95 (0-19-281854-6).

AMBROSE BIERCE
American. 1842–1914.

Bierce fought in the Civil War, was then a journalist, and eventually disappeared into Mexico, never to be heard from again. He left behind a body of powerful work—stories about the Civil War, stories about horror, stories just to generate humor—yet always in a formal, controlled hand; always with tight, rich sentences; always with an eye to satire. A Bierce story has psychological twists and turns that challenge preconceived notions of reality. A darkness, a haunted feeling, pervades his work, as if, like Poe, he wrote from a corner of his heart where light never reached. "An Occurrence at Owl Creek Bridge," about an execution of a soldier during the Civil War, features a startling ending.

Bierce, Ambrose. *The Complete Short Stories of Ambrose Bierce.* 496p. Univ. of Nebraska, paper, $10.95 (0-8032-6071-7).

JORGE LUIS BORGES
Argentine. 1899–1986.

A seminal figure in Latin American literature, Borges is certainly one of the few great twentieth-century fiction writers not to have written a novel; his high reputation rests upon his short stories alone. At the outset, the reader of Borges must surrender any predetermined ideas regarding what a story should be, for the man was a keen experimenter with form. A Borges tale may take the guise of a biographical essay or even a book review. Fantasy was his workplace; he upset reality in order to expose life's disorder. Written in a highly polished and evocative style, his works become vehicles for exploring intellectual concepts—creativity, the irrationality of the human mind, or the inability of humankind to accurately perceive truth or establish order in the world—rather than for depicting everyday events. "Tlon, Ugbar, Orbis Tertius," "The Library of Babel," "The South," and "Death and the Compass" are famous pieces—cerebral and singularly different from the work of other authors.

Borges, Jorge Luis. *Ficciones.* 174p. Grove, paper, $6.95 (0-394-17244-2).

ELIZABETH BOWEN
Anglo-Irish. 1899–1973.

The autobiographical *Bowen's Court* (1942) is a magnificent history of the author's English-descent land-owning family in Ireland's

County Cork. Bowen knew two worlds—England and the Ireland of the Anglo-Irish gentry—and she wrote about both in her stories. To enjoy Bowen, the reader must accept her style. Some perceive her writing as too rich, too convoluted for easy digestion; others find it readily embraceable—even exhilarating. Beyond that, a Bowen story is always furnished with roomfuls of luxurious detail. "Summer Night," for instance, is about a woman driving through a lovely, warm evening to rendezvous with her lover. The first two pages offer beautiful, scene-setting description that begs to be read and reread. Also notable are the ghostly "Demon Lover" and the intriguing "Happy Autumn Fields," with its unusual time shifts back and forth between World War II London and Victorian Ireland. Male-female relations and childhood were Bowen's forte.

> Bowen, Elizabeth. *The Collected Stories of Elizabeth Bowen.* 784p. Knopf, $20 (0-394-51666-4); Random, paper, $8.95 (0-394-75296-1).

ERSKINE CALDWELL
American. 1903–87.

The controversial author of the novels *Tobacco Road* (1932) and *God's Little Acre* (1933) has always borne a reputation for reveling in the seamy underside of poor southern life. Caldwell often wrote about the coarse relationship between poor rural black and white folks in the South in the early and middle parts of this century. He dealt with the sordid, baser aspects of human nature, eschewing well-roundedness in his characters in order to turn the reader's scrutiny to their grotesque sides. Yet his depictions are ironically impersonal and even humorous—he's not groaning and sweating over the plight of these pathetic people. Caldwell's style is simple yet exact, and, despite his notoriety for naughty humor, he was a dedicated writer, an even finer practitioner of the short story than the novel. "Candy-Man Beechum" is frequently anthologized. It's about a black mule skinner, going into town on a Saturday night to see his girl.

> Caldwell, Erskine. *The Black and White Stories of Erskine Caldwell.* 198p. Peachtree, $12.95 (0-931948-63-0).

WILLA CATHER
American. 1873–1947.

Virginia-born, but Nebraska-raised, Cather, through her Great Plains frontier experiences, filtered her courage-oriented sensibilities through warm-blooded yet dignified fiction. On one hand, she can be read for style alone. Elegant simplicity and perfect lucidity distinguish her prose. But the substance of her stories also touches the reader deeply. Cather wrote about hard lives, noble lives. Specifically, her work often deals with the conflicts faced in society by individuals of artistic sensitivity. "Paul's Case," her most famous tale, demonstrates this abiding theme well. (In fact, it is subtitled "A Study in Temperament.") Paul is a dreamy youth crushed to death by conformity.

> Cather, Willa. *Obscure Destinies*. 230p. Random, paper, $4.95 (0-394-71179-3).

> Cather, Willa. *The Old Beauty and Others*. 166p. Random, paper, $4.95 (0-394-72122-5).

> Cather, Willa. *The Troll Garden*. 160p. NAL, paper, $3.95 (0-452-00714-3).

JOHN CHEEVER
American. 1912–82.

Cheever was a chronicler of middle-class suburban America. In such stories as "O Youth and Beauty!" "The Swimmer," and "The Trouble of Marcie Flint," he used stiletto-sharp humor to expose the truth about suburbia's shady streets, pooled backyards, and that great battleground, the bedroom. Cheever knew instinctively the details of his characters' lives: what they said and ate and drank, how they were employed, and who they pretended to be and feared they actually were. He wrote with splendid eloquence—a gold mine for readers who thrill over an extensive vocabulary, intriguing syntax, and lush descriptions, ideas, and authorial commentary. Yet his stories don't seem overblown at all. Instead, they seem quite natural, as if someone very well spoken were relating the tales orally. It is amazingly easy to lose oneself in a Cheever story—and then to want to keep reading them one right after the other.

> Cheever, John. *The Stories of John Cheever*. 693p. Knopf, $20 (0-394-50087-3); Ballantine, paper, $3.50 (0-395-28436-4).

ANTON CHEKHOV
Russian. 1860–1904.

The supreme master—czar, perhaps?—of implication and suggestion, of telling stories by offering a nugget of information here and briefly sketching in a nuance there. Because of the keen significance of each of these selective details—rather than their cumulative impact—the reader comes to a quiet realization of just exactly what a character is all about. Chekhov's stories are gentle, humorous, poignant; but that doesn't mean they are insubstantial. They spring forth and crackle with real life, with as much vitality in the complex twentieth century as they did in the less-hurried nineteenth. Chekhov drew his material from all walks of Russian life—peasantry and aristocracy, men and women, military and bureaucracy. No one interested in short stories, especially in *writing* a short story, should miss "The Lady with the Pet Dog" or "Gooseberries." These are, like nearly every Chekhov tale, masterpieces of sensitive rendering of human nature, of sympathetic views of the narrownesses of human thought and behavior.

Chekhov, Anton. *The Russian Master and Other Stories.* 233p. Oxford, paper, $3.95 (0-19-281680-2).

KATE CHOPIN
American. 1851–1904.

Kate Chopin is an interesting literary case. A member of a socially prominent family in St. Louis, she married a Louisiana cotton broker and plantation owner. Left a widow early, she returned to St. Louis, and there began a writing career. Her novel *The Awakening* was published in 1899. Its frank sensuality was roundly vilified, and Chopin's literary reputation went into a tailspin. But recently this splendid novel has been recognized as a masterpiece and is being taught in the college classroom. A readership is growing for her short stories as well. They are set in the Louisiana Chopin came to know as a married woman, among the Creoles and Cajuns. She focused particularly on women's wants and needs in marriage, treating love and sexuality with psychological incisiveness, abiding sensuality, but with moral objectivity. Chopin's approach was realistic, her sentences economically rendered, with each word chosen for its opalescence. The brief "Desiree's Baby" is a staggering tale about racial mixing.

Chopin, Kate. *The Awakening and Selected Short Stories.* 211p. Bantam, paper, $2.95 (0-553-21194-3).

JOSEPH CONRAD
Polish-born, naturalized British. 1857–1924.

Conrad went to sea as a teenager, and his experiences gave him much to write about. (Amazingly, English was an acquired language.) His long tales are powerful and exciting portraits of men facing adversity—nature's brutal elements or man's inhumanity to man—and what it takes to overcome it. Conjuring up the right atmosphere was crucial to Conrad's vision. What's in the air often brings out what's in the character. Nuance of expression was not his style. Instead, he created big, bold images, with every sentence carrying great pictorial weight. A Conrad story is quite vivid, then. The reader is virtually sucked into the scene depicted in "Heart of Darkness"—up the Congo River, where the protagonist has discovered, and is overcome by, humanity's hidden carnivorous nature.

Conrad, Joseph. *Great Short Works of Joseph Conrad.* 407p. Harper, paper, $3.80 (0-06-083039-5).

A. E. COPPARD
English. 1878–1957.

Coppard was self-taught in literature and didn't publish until later than most fiction writers. He never wrote a novel, yet his stories serve as guide to the English countryside, introducing to the reader a bevy of quietly noble folk. There is a fablelike—a folkloric—simple dignity to his work. On the surface, Coppard's sentences seem to be artlessly straightforward, but then it becomes clear that each phrase has been cut like an expensive gem, with perfect facets reflecting sheer poetic beauty. Coppard is best read slowly, in order to feel his vigor, his power, his exquisite sensitivity. "Dusky Ruth" is an exemplary tale.

Coppard, A. E. *The Collected Tales of A. E. Coppard.* 532p. Ayer, $40 (0-405-08119-7).

STEPHEN CRANE
American. 1871–1900.

"None of them knew the color of the sky." That's the opening line of Crane's famous story about shipwreck, "The Open Boat." Who could possibly resist, after reading that brief but potent sentence, wanting to find out who these people are and why they aren't noticing the sky above them? Crane led an adventurous life, one that was not entirely respectable. Critics still argue whether he was a realist, a naturalist, or an impressionist. That debate is specious, however. Simply relish Crane's use of varied settings: urban centers, the West, the locales he encountered as a war correspondent. Crane dealt with big moral and life-and-death issues, and no matter how his technique is categorized, he remains a clear, precise, indelible, even lovely writer. "The Blue Hotel" and "The Bride Comes to Yellow Sky" form, with "The Open Boat," a trio of his most frequently anthologized, and best, stories.

> Crane, Stephen. *Stories and Tales*. 350p. Random, paper, $2.95 (0-394-70010-4).

WALTER DE LA MARE
English. 1873–1956.

De la Mare wrote in a grand, bold, decorated, unrestrained style, not designed for carefree reading. His tales of horror, fantasy, and the supernatural feature plots built on involved frameworks, which require patience in absorbing them one step at a time. Nevertheless, they're marvelous works. Taking a typical English setting, in town or country—a house, a garden, a railway station—de la Mare injects some kind of insidious evil or unnaturalness. A sense of foreboding is followed by increased suspense—and the reader remains haunted long after the story has been finished. "The House" is a good example of the author's chilling style. A man who knows he's dying tours his own domicile for the very last time.

> De la Mare, Walter. *Best Stories of Walter de la Mare*. 397p. Faber and Faber, paper, $7.95 (0-571-13076-3).

ISAK DINESEN
Danish. 1885–1962.

Isak Dinesen was the pseudonym of Karen Blixen, whose life was brought to widespread public attention with the 1985 movie version of her autobiographical narrative, *Out of Africa,* which starred Meryl Streep and Robert Redford. Blixen married a distant cousin, a Swedish baron, and in 1913 they went to East Africa to found a coffee plantation. It was not an uncomplicated venture; divorced, having left the plantation forever, Blixen returned home to Denmark and began writing for financial reasons. Her stories are fables and fairy tales— unabashed expositions of the travails of kings, queens, nobles, and fashionable society in love and in lust or embroiled in adventures or calamities caused by nature or the supernatural. The settings are the historical past, with lots of threatening atmosphere and plenty of costumes and written in a baroque style. But beneath the romantic facades there lurks a very precise, sensitive, and delicate understanding of the nuances of character. Finely carved and shaded personalities exist behind the gothic trappings of a Dinesen story. A prime example is "The Deluge at Norderney," a long, involved tale concerning a storm in 1835, which wreaks havoc on the lives of certain individuals at a Danish resort. It's a wonderful psychological fathoming.

> Dinesen, Isak. *Seven Gothic Tales.* 420p. Modern Library, $6.95 (0-394-60496-2).

WILLIAM FAULKNER
American. 1897–1962.

Faulkner created one of literature's most fully realized, enduring worlds. You can visit the fictional Yoknapatawpha County by way of his novels and his stories. The latter offer a less-circuitous itinerary, which is to say that his notoriously convoluted plots are less full-blown and thus less an obstruction to appreciating Yoknapatawpha and its populace. Faulkner was fascinated with the shift from Old South to New, with the degeneration of the families of gentility, with human nature's propensity for perversion, and with the absurdity in the lives of eccentric people. The very accessible "Dry September" gives clear indication of the depth of his passionate—even obsessive—feeling for the South.

> Faulkner, William. *Collected Stories of William Faulkner.* 900p. Random, $22.95 (0-394-41967-7); paper, $8.95 (0-394-72257-4).

RUDOLPH FISHER
American. 1902–67.

Fisher was a stellar contributor to the Harlem Renaissance, the black cultural movement centered in Harlem in the 1920s. He is little read today, unfortunately, but his short stories should prove fascinating to anyone interested in the form or in black culture in the interwar period. Fisher was a practicing physician and a writer simultaneously, but his stories are definitely not the product of a Sunday dabbler. The rhythmic cadences of his style and his stance toward his race—at once humorous, sensitive, and prideful but not defensive—work together to make these pieces about the lives of ordinary folks both eminently artful and exceptionally inviting. Fisher wrote of black people recently arrived in Harlem and getting used to its streets and attitudes; and he wrote of well-worn Harlemites whose bodies and souls suffered no less than those of the newcomers. "John Archer's Nose," a detective story, is particularly appealing.

> Fisher, Rudolph. *The City of Refuge: The Collected Stories of Rudolph Fisher.* 196p. Univ. of Missouri, $25 (0-8262-0630-1).

F. SCOTT FITZGERALD
American. 1896–1940.

"Let me tell you about the very rich. They are different from you and me," says Fitzgerald in his story "The Rich Boy." In effect a social historian of the Jazz Age, Fitzgerald became legendary for living fast, for writing about the moneyed class, for burning out quickly. Many of his stories were cranked out for quick, consumer-magazine publication, mainly to put money into his pocket. But all of them are still worth reading as greatly entertaining jaunts back to a time that continues to hold fascination. The lives of men and women in and out of sync with each other preoccupied Fitzgerald, and he served up his little dramas with a glib tone and ingratiatingly clever style. "May Day" and "The Diamond as Big as the Ritz" are more profound than most of his works.

> Fitzgerald, F. Scott. *The Stories of F. Scott Fitzgerald.* 512p. Scribner, $27.50 (0-684-15366-1); paper, $9.95 (0-684-71737-9).

GUSTAVE FLAUBERT
French. 1821–80.

Flaubert is celebrated for his realism—his mastery at depicting ordinary people (from servants to professionals) and their normal experiences as well as very realistic descriptions of exotic settings. He is also acclaimed for his perfection of style: careful attention was paid to every sentence he wrote. Flaubert wrote about love, faith, and sensuousness, painting rich verbal pictures that imparted to the reader just how things looked, felt to the touch, or sounded and smelled. His most admired short story is "The Simple Heart." To purists who insist a short story should entail only an isolated moment, this piece will seem to be a condensed novel, with too many episodes over too long a time frame to qualify as a "real" short story. It remains a moving portrayal of the life of the good maidservant, Félicité.

Flaubert, Gustave. *Three Tales*. 124p. Penguin, paper, $2.95 (0-14-044106-9).

MARY E. WILKINS FREEMAN
American. 1852–1930.

Freeman is labeled a "local colorist," but that shouldn't imply that her New England–based stories are harmless, humorous little sketches rendered in the fewest and faintest of brushstrokes, with appeal limited to people familiar with the area. The truth of the matter is that Freeman's stories transcend both the time in which they take place—the late nineteenth century—and their locale to speak to readers of today. She wrote about granite-hard New England women of the countryside and small towns, characters of resistance and resilience in the face of hard climate, hard soil, hard men. Freeman realistically limned the interiors of these women's lives, carefully insinuating a comprehension of their strengths of will. All of this is delivered in a crystalline style. In "The Revolt of 'Mother,' " Mother is upset with Father for building another barn when what they really need is a bigger house. So she moves the family into the newly completed barn while he's away.

Freeman, Mary E. Wilkins. *Selected Stories of Mary E. Wilkins Freeman*. 344p. Norton, paper, $5.95 (0-393-30106-0).

CAROLINE GORDON
American. 1895–1981.

Gordon and her husband, poet Allen Tate, were participants in the so-called Southern Renaissance—the rise to superior status of a number of southern U.S. writers in the first half of this century. Gordon, born in Kentucky, wrote about the land and what it produced, and about the families who lived on it and their ties to each other. She was obsessively southern, and her writing is abidingly concerned with the order and dignity of the South's agrarian past and the social confusion she saw in its industrial present. Gordon was a psychological writer, an analyzer of relationships and their causations, conditions, consequences. She maintained a poised, unobtrusive use of history—the Civil War, particularly—in some of her stories, such as "Hear the Nightingale Sing." The fact that they are set in the past is important to their premises, not because Gordon was contriving an artificial stage on which to conduct a costume drama. "Old Red," Gordon's most famous story, shows her to be a dexterous painter of detail. It features a protagonist Gordon uses in other fictional works, Professor Aleck Maury, who loves to fish.

> Gordon, Caroline. *The Collected Stories of Caroline Gordon.* 352p. Farrar, $17.95 (0-374-12630-5); paper, $10.95 (0-374-51675-8).

NATHANIEL HAWTHORNE
American. 1804–64.

Born in the old town of Salem, Massachusetts, the highly intelligent Hawthorne mined the historical past for material and delved into the supernatural for powerful effect. His very psychological stories deal with good and evil; he probes moral issues and reports his findings in terms of black and white, with very little gray shading. Nonetheless, Hawthorne remains one of the most compelling of early American contributors to the story genre. He relied heavily on the use of symbol and allegory: the symbols are organic to the stories and thus work without actually having to be recognized as such by the reader; and ignoring the allegorical levels simply means they can still be enjoyed for their rich but very controlled language and their eerie drama. "Ethan Brand" and "Rappaccini's Daughter" are prime examples of Hawthorne's multilevel expression.

> Hawthorne, Nathaniel. *Tales and Sketches.* 1,493p. Library of America, $27.50 (0-940450-03-8).

ERNEST HEMINGWAY
American. 1899–1961.

Clean, simple sentences. Hemingway is famous for them. And for writing about male bravado in the face of adversity. The truth of the matter is, anyone interested in learning the fundamentals of expressive writing would do well to study each and every sentence in Hemingway's short stories. He's had imitators, but none have come close to his sheer eloquence. As far as his obsession with hairy-chested men and their courage under pressure—well, that can pose a slight irritation to the reader initially, but it is never a permanent impediment to the enjoyment of his writing. His stories are, without a doubt, arresting in their abrupt accuracy of speech and manner and psychology; and underneath his seemingly chauvinistic stances, Hemingway could show sensitivity to insecurities. Sports activities, the out-of-doors, violent death, war: these were Hemingway's preoccupations. Stories such as "Big Two-Hearted River" and "The Killers" show how well he knew these physical/emotional terrains.

Hemingway, Ernest. *The Short Stories of Ernest Hemingway.* 499p. Scribner, paper, $10.95 (0-684-71806-5).

O. HENRY
American. 1862–1910.

O. Henry, pseudonym of William Sydney Porter, was the supreme practitioner of the trick ending, the ironic twist, which, rather than putting a nice cap on the story, slaps the reader in the face with a complete surprise. Not a particularly admirable device, it can too often hide slipshod narrative development—which in O. Henry's case it often did. Nevertheless, O. Henry greatly popularized the short story, gave it strength in the public's mind as something perfectly suited to satisfying the need to be entertained. On the other hand, his knowledge of real people—whether those found in New York or out West or in Latin America—was thorough and sensitive, and there's an authenticity to his writing that is to be admired. "The Gift of the Magi" shows the trick ending at work, but the story leaves you moved as well.

Henry, O. *The Pocket Book of O. Henry Stories.* 238p. Washington Square, paper, $3.95 (0-671-55697-5).

E. T. A. HOFFMANN
German. 1776–1822.

Hoffmann held membership in the German branch of the Romantic movement, which swept European literature and art in the eighteenth and nineteenth centuries. Adherents believed in the essential goodness of humankind and in the primacy of nature and of the senses over civilization and reason. Romanticism led Hoffmann, along with many other practitioners, inside himself—to explore, in his works, dreams and fantasy (fairy tales, tales of the macabre). Thus, he wrote of aberrant individuals, strange situations, supernatural conditions. His characters might be artists outside mainstream society, or even split personalities. Hoffmann's diction is old-fashioned in its formality, though his insights into haunted corners of the mind are as immaculately on target as the day they were written. "Mademoiselle de Scuderi," long but fast moving, is a detective story set in Paris during the reign of Louis XIV, centering on a robbery-and-murder spree that has the city terrorized. Hoffmann's influence on Edgar Allan Poe is well in evidence in this tale.

>Hoffmann, E. T. A. *Tales of E. T. A. Hoffman.* 279p. Univ. of Chicago, paper, $9.95 (0-226-34789-3).

LANGSTON HUGHES
American. 1902–67.

Hughes was one of the most significant twentieth-century black writers. In addition to short stories, he was also accomplished in the novel, drama, poetry, and autobiography. He wrote of black people in Harlem, in farming regions, in Florida—all over the country—and focused on the raw edge of black-and-white relations. Hughes distilled the various bruisings involved in the black experience in this country, but his point of view isolated black pride as well. He wrote not with vitriol but in the honest pursuit of truth. Many of Hughes' stories feature Jesse B. Semple, called Simple, a streetwise Harlemite brimming with tales and home-spun philosophy. The obvious humor aside, the Simple stories are forceful depictions of Harlem life and, by representation, the universal black experience. "Little Dog" is not a Simple story, but one in a serious vein concerning a white woman who obtains a dog and has the black janitor get meat for it every day. In time, it is the janitor, not the dog, whom the woman longs to see when she gets home from work. A disturbing situation, and a disturbing tale.

>Hughes, Langston. *The Ways of White Folks.* 248p. Random, paper, $4.95 (0-394-71304-4).

WASHINGTON IRVING
American. 1783–1859.

Irving was the first writer in the new American nation to gain stature abroad. Most of his work is not all that exciting these days, with the exception of two stories from *The Sketch Book of Geoffrey Crayon, Gent.*—"Rip Van Winkle," who, of course, fell asleep for twenty years and awakened as an old man; and "The Legend of Sleepy Hollow," the famous tale of schoolmaster Ichabod Crane and the headless horseman. These two stories should be read by everyone; they retain great charm. Irving wrote them in a style that is graceful, exacting, colorful. For example, the description of Ichabod Crane:

He was tall, but exceedingly lank, with narrow shoulders, long arms and legs, hands that dangled a mile out of his sleeves, feet that might have served for shovels, and his whole frame most loosely hung together. His head was small, and flat at top, with huge ears, large green glassy eyes, and a long snipe nose, so that it looked like a weathercock, perched upon his spindle neck, to tell which way the wind blew. To see him striding along the profile of a hill on a windy day, with his clothes bagging and fluttering about him, one might have mistaken him for the genius of famine descending upon the earth, or some scarecrow eloped from a cornfield.

Irving, Washington. *Sketch Book*. 379p. NAL, paper, $2.95 (0-451-51614-1).

CHRISTOPHER ISHERWOOD
English-born, naturalized American. 1904–86.

Isherwood wrote that he went to Berlin in 1929 because "Berlin meant Boys." The result of his familiarity with that city and its denizens was a cycle of sharp-edged yet ironically elegiac stories about Germany on the brink of the Nazi abyss. Isherwood was fascinated by the cultural-political breakdown Berlin was undergoing during the last years of the Weimar Republic and by the colorful people who stood out above the crowd but were not heroic in any ordinary sense of the word. From this social tension, he spun his Berlin stories, refraining from overt judgment, but nevertheless presenting a rich tapestry of subjective observations of sex and society in interwar Berlin. In crisp dialogue, every person who populates these stories leaves an indelible impression on the reader—particularly the main character of the totally enchanting story "Sally Bowles." The Broadway play and later movie *Cabaret* was based on Isherwood's stories.
   Isherwood, Christopher. *The Berlin Stories*. 207p. New Directions, paper, $6.95 (0-8112-0070-1).

HENRY JAMES
American-born, naturalized British. 1843–1916.

He had no choice in being born an American, of course, but James *did* choose where to spend his adult life: in Europe, primarily England. Consequently, the differences in American and European cultures were always on his mind; and the clash between New World manners and morals and those of the Old occupied much of his writing—as did the artist's difficult place in the insensitive world outside art. James is a literary giant—no, a god—of whom readers are often afraid because of his reputation for density of prose style and ambiguity of point. Granted, his last novels are close to impenetrable; but he is incontestably an artist of the highest order, and the experience of reading his work should not be missed by any discriminating lover of literature. Approach James through his short stories and long short stories (novellas, really), in which he showed all of his talents more directly than in his novels. "The Real Thing" (in *Daisy Miller and Other Stories*) offers sensitivity, lack of obscurity, and even charm, displaying James's outstanding gifts for giving perfect shape to a story and understanding human nature. Move on to a longer piece such as "The Aspern Papers," wherein lies James's undeniably compelling power. High art, yes; but behind the rather grand facades of James's stories stands perfectly proportioned psychological portraits.

James, Henry. *The Aspern Papers* and *The Turn of the Screw.* 270p. Penguin, paper, $2.50 (0-14-043224-8).

James, Henry. *Daisy Miller and Other Stories.* 192p. Penguin, paper, $2.50 (0-14-006721-3).

James, Henry. *The Figure in the Carpet and Other Stories.* 453p. Penguin, paper, $5.95 (0-14-043255-8).

James, Henry. *An International Episode and Other Stories.* 239p. Penguin, paper, $4.95 (0-14-043227-2).

SARAH ORNE JEWETT
American. 1849–1909.

The talents of Sarah Orne Jewett will amend the view of anyone who thinks any fiction writer of the nineteenth century is bound to be dry or flowery or artificial or steeped in convoluted sentence building. There is a clarity and directness to her writing that guides the reader easily through her stories. Jewett, from New England stock, wrote about the harsh beauty of the Maine landscape and the resourcefulness of the people who lived there—regular people, fishing and farming folk. A local colorist, a regionalist, Jewett nevertheless drew characters that have appeal outside the confines of their geographical perimeters. *The Country of the Pointed Firs* is her most famous work. Sometimes thought of as an episodic novel, it is actually a cycle of stories about a woman who goes to spend the summer in the little Maine coastal town of Dunnett Landing. Through vignettes and sketches the reader comes to know the people and the sounds and smells of the place. Jewett has a wonderfully accurate ear for dialogue, for the New England dialect. She portrays these basic, hardworking people with a pinch of satire but also with a great deal of compassion and understanding. Jewett wrote many other stories besides the *Pointed Firs* sequence. One of the best is "The Only Rose," in which Mrs. Bickford tries to decide on which of the graves of her three husbands she will place her single rose.

Jewett, Sarah Orne. *The Country of the Pointed Firs and Other Stories.* 336p. Norton, paper, $7.96 (0-393-00048-6).

JAMES JOYCE
Irish. 1882–1941.

Joyce is certainly one of the greatest literary figures of all time. While his novels may intimidate many readers, his stories should not. *The Dubliners* is the one volume of stories he wrote. These stories render key moments in ordinary, uninspired middle-class lives in the Irish capital, but in far less arcane prose than that of his novels. These carefully worded tales are far from shallow, prowling deep into seemingly still psychological waters. *The Dubliners* is a cycle, a unit; taken together, in the order Joyce arranged them, the stories present a pattern of major phases through which the human life passes, from childhood onward. Little happens in Joyce's stories in terms of plot; they're more about states of mind than fast action. These Dubliners' lives are generally cheerless. But one turns to Joyce for profundity of communication. The best story in the collection, "The Dead," is universally considered by critics to be one of the most beautifully executed stories in the English language. It requires more than one reading to gather its full measure of wisdom about the human condition.

Joyce, James. *The Dubliners.* 224p. Modern Library, $5.95 (0-394-60464-4); 223p. Penguin, paper, $2.95 (0-14-004222-9).

FRANZ KAFKA
Czech. 1883–1924.

Reading Kafka is disquieting. His peculiar visions of inner life, as depicted in his stories, strike the reader as paradigmatic of the enigmas of twentieth-century life at large. Born in Prague, once a city within the borders of the Austro-Hungarian empire, Kafka died early, with his fame coming posthumously. He was abidingly concerned with the separateness of the individual—the emotional distance between a person and his or her familial, social, and political communities. His stories (written in German) have a dreamlike quality, almost nightmarish, though his spartan style is easily read. Kafka's work often reflects the universal unsettledness and fears of isolation. "In the Penal Colony," a story about an apparatus for executions, is unforgettable.

Kafka, Franz. *The Complete Stories.* 486p. Schocken, $14.50 (0-8052-3419-5); paper, $7.95 (0-8052-0423-7).

RUDYARD KIPLING
English. 1865–1936.

While it may come as a surprise to those who think of him only as a writer for children, Rudyard Kipling is, generally speaking, ranked very high as a short-story writer. Some critics insist he's the best Britain has produced. Despite occasional and uncomfortable lapses into what certainly seems like racist talk, Kipling's stories are every bit as exciting and intellectually stimulating as they were decades ago. He wrote of India and England and other global locales as well as all kinds of people and their predicaments. Kipling handled dialogue brilliantly, particularly dialect, which often leaves his stories somewhat difficult to follow. (In fact, his later stories are abstruse.) But careful reading will reveal perfect—and perfectly sophisticated—gems of compact character and well-delineated atmosphere. Kipling stories simultaneously entertain and challenge. "Mrs. Bathurst" is his most celebrated, but there are many others equally enjoyable. "The Man Who Would Be King" is irresistible.

Kipling, Rudyard. *A Choice of Kipling's Prose.* Craig Raine, ed. 448p. Faber and Faber, $22.95 (0-571-13735-0); paper, $10.95 (0-571-13850-0).

RING LARDNER
American. 1885–1933.

Lardner came to story writing from sportswriting. A great humorist and master of the vernacular, Lardner proficiently reconstructed on the printed page just how plain folks really talked, thus exerting a great influence on fiction writers coming after him. Beneath the jocularity—behind the use of everyday, up-and-down-Main-Street diction—Lardner lays common people open with razor-sharp satire. The overall effect, despite the humor flying off in all directions, is surgically precise. "The Golden Honeymoon," about an old married couple gone to Florida for their golden anniversary, is both hilarious and insightful.

> Lardner, Ring. *Haircut and Other Stories.* 192p. Random, paper, $5.95 (0-394-72610-3).

D. H. LAWRENCE
English. 1885–1930.

While Lawrence was one of the greatest novelists in the English language, his greatness also extends to the short story. Repressed sexuality, unspoken passion—these Lawrence wrote about voluptuously in his many stories, but in a more direct, concentrated—and thus in many readers' eyes, more effective—form than in his novels. Lawrence was the antithesis of Henry James in that he was uninterested in any sort of "artistic" considerations when it came to giving his stories shape and contour. Lawrence wants the reader to stand up close and feel the texture of the paint he's used, whereas James wants you to stand back and admire the composition and the way the picture was matted and framed. "The Odour of Chrysanthemums" is so very Lawrentian. The wife of a coal miner is brought her husband's dead body, and only then, after he's been washed and laid out, does she really *see* him. A lovely tale.

> Lawrence, D. H. *Complete Short Stories of D. H. Lawrence.* 3v. 853p. Penguin, paper. v.1: $3.95 (0-14-004382-9); v.2: $4.95 (0-14-004255-5); v.3: $3.95 (0-14-004383-7).

JACK LONDON
American. 1876–1916.

London led a short, unrestrained life. He wrote sinewy adventure stories, often set in the Yukon, which center on heroic individuals at odds with the forces of nature. But underneath the heavy musculature in a London story is a rough elegance, a hard sensuality—not unlike a brawny football player dancing ballet, doing well at it, and enjoying it. London's ability to maintain a keen tension from first page to last, in every story, draws the reader in fully. "To Build a Fire" is quintessential London: a man out in the hostile elements, dog at his side, death looking him square in the face.

> London, Jack. *To Build a Fire and Other Stories.* 389p. Bantam, paper, $3.95 (0-553-21213-3).

BERNARD MALAMUD
American. 1914–86.

With lapses into abject fantasy, which leave his stories with an enticing, rewarding fablelike tenor, Malamud was most successful writing about New York Jews, his characters ranging from a student to an art historian to a frozen-foods salesman. Human suffering, religious intolerance, and the power of love are a few of the themes found in Malamud's deceptively simple stories. In "The Jewbird," one of his most famous tales, a blackbird flies one hot August evening into the open kitchen window of the New York apartment of Harry Cohen and his wife and son. The bird talks—not just mimicking human voice, but actually showing capability of reasoning and carrying on conversation—then sticks around and tries to become part of the family. This short work is disarmingly charming and devastatingly wry; and beneath the uncomplicated veneer is an allegorical level: Harry's rough treatment of the bird is a paradigm for anti-Semitism as practiced by Gentiles and other Jews.

Malamud, Bernard. *The Stories of Bernard Malamud.* 350p. NAL, paper, 7.95 (0-452-25585-6).

KATHERINE MANSFIELD
New Zealander. 1888–1923.

Born and raised in a far corner of the British Empire, Mansfield spent her adult life in England and on the Continent. In her stories, she drew upon her experiences in all these places, particularly her native New Zealand. She often wrote about lonely, emotionally isolated women and about wide-eyed children gathering impressions of adults. Mansfield's distinctive narrative voice is resonantly understated, showing a remarkable adeptness at moving smoothly in and out of a character's consciousness. (This seemed quite experimental at the time she was writing, though it is a standard fictional technique these days.) Some contemporary critics feel Mansfield's work is too precious and ephemeral; nevertheless, sensitive readers will see that the focus she places on the tender moments in peoples' lives illuminates the vulnerabilities of all of us. "The Wrong House" is her keenest piece, a stunning depiction of an old woman's reaction to a hearse mistakenly paying a call at her door.

Mansfield, Katherine. *Short Stories of Katherine Mansfield.* 688p. Ecco, paper, $11.95 (0-88001-025-8).

W. SOMERSET MAUGHAM
English. 1874–1965.

Maugham was very popular in his day and is certainly still read enjoyably today. He traveled to the far corners of the earth, and his stories reflect the experiences he garnered on these trips. Maugham's stories feature definite beginnings, middles, and endings, and their very traditional structure is upholstered in rich—often exotic—detail, all wrapped up in an engaging, urbane tone. Maugham wrote, fundamentally, about how people do or do not get along, what's underneath their attraction or disdain for each other. That doesn't mean he's a profound analyzer of personality; he is simply a careful observer of behavior. Maugham's stories are always good dramas, though, with very distinctive characters. The famous "Rain," about the South-Seas floozy Sadie Thompson, "The Letter," and "The Outstation" are all compelling.

> Maugham, W. Somerset. *Collected Short Stories*. 4v. Penguin, paper. v.1: 441p., $4.95 (0-14-001871-9); v.2: 424p., $4.95 (0-14-001872-7); v.3: 256p., $4.95 (0-14-001873-5); v.4: 464p., $4.95 (0-14-001874-3).

GUY DE MAUPASSANT
French. 1850–93.

Prolific and straightforward, Maupassant wrote volumes of realistic stories about lives not always on the up-and-up—the peasant folk of his native Normandy, soldiers, small-potatoes functionaries. Chekhov is professor emeritus of the school whereby story writers sample the core of a character and a situation, with little in the way of preface or introduction, and no tidy ending. Maupassant, on the other hand, preferred to compose stories that guide the reader from the shallow to the deep end and then back onto dry land. That is not to suggest Maupassant's stories are slow and tedious; on the contrary, there is not a wasted word, and a lot of action is pressed into small space. He lays open the bare essence of a character with a steady hand—what each one is really like stripped of disguise, as it were—with nothing left ambiguous. It's always obvious in a Maupassant story what's going on and how and why it ended the way it did. "The Necklace" is his most famous tale.

> Maupassant, Guy de. *Selected Short Stories*. 368p. Penguin, paper, $4.95 (0-14-044243-X).

CARSON MC CULLERS
American. 1917–67.

McCullers died early, at age 50, leaving behind a not particularly extensive body of literature—but a fine one. McCullers was southern, and like her contemporary, Flannery O'Connor, another notable southern practitioner of the short story, McCullers wrote about grotesques, people afflicted physically and emotionally. Her themes include loneliness and the mental anguish that stems from love gone awry. Her unadorned style is quietly rigorous, her tales both charming and disquieting—an absorbing challenge. But further comparisons with Flannery O'Connor and other significant southern short-story writers reveal psychological portraiture less fully realized and ironic observations less well phrased. (After O'Connor, McCullers is most often compared to Katherine Anne Porter and Eudora Welty.) Nevertheless, the long "Ballad of the Sad Cafe" is an established and undeniably successful work. Cousin Lyman, a hunchbacked dwarf, walks into Miss Amelia Evans's eating and drinking establishment one day. The love relationship that ensues changes the cafe into a new place—but not forever. This peculiar, haunting story views grotesqueness of the body and the mind from a not unsympathetic stance.

McCullers, Carson. *Collected Stories.* 392p. Houghton, $18.95 (0-395-44179-X); paper, $11.95 (0-395-44243-5).

GEORGE MOORE
Irish. 1852–1933.

It is a shame Moore is little read these days. He is of major significance in Irish literature, one of the supreme masters of the short story in the English language. Intending to be a painter, Moore eventually became involved in the turn-of-the-century renaissance of Irish culture. Out of his concern over fostering a native Irish literature came the cycle of stories *The Untilled Field,* a series of satiric depictions of Irish life, of typical people of the village and countryside. The later *Story-Teller's Holiday* is a remarkable book, a tour-de-force, presenting a body of tales woven together into one long, virtually seamless narrative. (It's a book best read from cover to cover, not dipping in here and there.) Moore's stories are psychologically deep and culturally exact, demonstrating why he is considered one of the finest stylists ever.

Moore, George. *Story-Teller's Holiday.* Liveright, $7.95 (0-87140-869-4).

Moore, George. *The Untilled Field.* Ayers, $15 (0-8369-3600-0).

FLANNERY O'CONNOR
American. 1925–64.

Out of the soil and citizenry of her native Georgia, O'Connor drew material for her stories. She is famous for the violence she depicts, for her dark humor, and for her abiding religious concern (i.e., the hows and whys of existence outside of divine grace, and the human battle to regain it). Everywhere O'Connor looked she saw individuals who were morally impaired and physically imperfect. These were not lives high in substance and purpose, yet she wrote about them in a tragicomic vein. The reader laughs yet with understanding. O'Connor possessed a marvelous ear for dialogue; her style was straightforward, rock-solid. "A Good Man Is Hard to Find" is vintage O'Connor, about a family on an automobile trip to Florida. Along a rough country road, the car takes a flip, and the family is . . . yes, it's true, wiped out by a gang of desperadoes who happen along!

O'Connor, Flannery. *The Complete Stories.* 555p. Farrar, $25 (0-374-12752-2); paper, $8.95 (0-374-51536-0).

FRANK O'CONNOR
Irish. 1903–66.

SEAN O'FAOLAIN
Irish. 1900–85.

LIAM O'FLAHERTY
Irish. 1896–1984.

Of the same generation, this triumvirate accomplished lasting results as they carried the torch of Irish short-story writing handed them from George Moore and James Joyce and passed it on to contemporary Irish story writers.

With marvelous humor and poignancy, O'Connor wrote stories in a personal tone, as if he were actually sitting down and spinning a yarn aloud. There is an immediacy in his writing, a sense of the shared anecdote passed down to the next generation. He evokes with inherent articulateness the atmosphere of provincial Ireland, rendering indelibly the nature of the populace, from children to old folks. O'Connor created wonderful, idiosyncratic characters who handle the problems in their rough lives very much in their own fashion. Read "Guests of the Nation" to see how Irish politics imbued his writing, "The Drunkard" for its humor, and "The Long Road to Ummera" to be moved to tears.

O'Faolain's stories are a lot less like yarns than O'Connor's. O'Faolain stands back a bit, in order to gain a clearer analytical perspective of the socioeconomic/political environment of Ireland. His characters are more finely chiseled, the atmosphere and psychology slightly keener, his style more lovely in its imagery. O'Faolain is, then, the finer artist of the two—but perhaps less charming than O'Connor. "Lovers of the Lake" is among his most popular and most rewarding stories. It's about a man and woman—lovers—who go on a pilgrimage.

Of the three, O'Flaherty is generally the briefer, denser, more poetic writer. Without much development of scene and character, he goes in for the hard punch, delivered in sharp language. O'Flaherty offers quick dramas set in ordinary domestic surroundings, in drab communities, within lives led with no luxury and at the mercy of the elements. He's more instinctual than O'Faolain and O'Connor—writing more from the guts than with heart or mind. Uniquely, and without schmaltz or contrivance, O'Flaherty crafted some tales that feature animals as main characters. "The Wounded Cormorant" is one of the best of these.

> O'Connor, Frank. *Collected Stories.* 702p. Knopf, $20 (0-394-51602-8); Random, paper, $8.95 (0-394-71048-7).

> O'Faolain, Sean. *The Collected Stories of Sean O'Faolain.* 1,312p. Little, $29.95 (0-316-63294-5).

> O'Flaherty, Liam. *The Wounded Cormorant and Other Stories.* 256p. Norton, $5.95 (0-393-00704-9).

JOHN O'HARA
American. 1905–70.

Some critics deem O'Hara one of the best short-story writers the United States has produced; others see his fiction as just good journalism. Either way, he has proved abidingly popular. O'Hara wrote many stories over a long career. Dialogue is the most important aspect of his stories—he always got the vocabulary, phonetics, cadences, and syntax just right, no matter what the socioeconomic group, from the moneyed class to the upper-middle class, to ordinary working people and even show-business types. This skill enabled him to conjure a vivid character in brief space. O'Hara supplemented his ear for dialogue with a keen consciousness of social trappings, for instance, the cars, the neighborhoods, the kinds of dwellings. He was very much in touch with the mores of many walks of American life. Regardless whether a story such as "The Doctor's Son" is art or simply accurate reportage, it can't be denied that O'Hara is eminently easy to read, to understand, to be entertained by.

>   O'Hara, John. *Collected Stories of John O'Hara.* 414p. Random, $19.95 (0-394-54083-2); paper, $9.95 (0-394-74311-3).

EDGAR ALLAN POE
American. 1809–49.

Poe makes a good vocabulary lesson—the reader is bound to head for the dictionary at some point while reading him. But that's not to imply that reading Poe is to engage in work, nor to imply that he's good-for-you-thus-must-be-dry-as-dust. On the contrary, Poe's stories of detection, of horror, of adventure, of science fiction, while historically important in the evolution of the short story, remain vital reading today. The darkness of Poe's soul pervades all of his stories, leaving them disturbing yet undeniably absorbing. Atmosphere was his strong suit; the threatening feeling he stirred into so many of his stories fairly wafts off every page and into the reader's senses. "The Tell-Tale Heart" is arguably the best short story of its kind in the English language.

>   Poe, Edgar Allan. *Selected Tales.* 316p. Oxford, paper, $2.95 (0-19-281522-9).

KATHERINE ANNE PORTER
American. 1890–1980.

Porter lived a long while but published relatively little. Nevertheless, what she may have lacked in quantity she more than compensated for in quality. Porter is often referred to as a writer's writer because of the shimmering beauty of her seemingly effortless style and her graceful use of symbol. Consequently, she deserves a much wider readership than many other writers. Porter was from the South and traveled in— and adored—Mexico. She effectively transferred onto the written page her deeply held reactions to these places. The sequence of very short stories called "The Old Order" leaves an indelible impression of her deep emotional commitment to her family's past within the context of the passing of the gentility of the late-nineteenth-century Old South.

Porter, Katherine Anne. *The Collected Stories of Katherine Anne Porter.* 495p. HBJ, paper, $7.95 (0-15-618876-7).

JEAN RHYS
West Indian. 1894–1979.

Born and raised on the Caribbean island of Dominica, Rhys spent her adult life mostly in England and France; her stories are generally set in those locales. Rhys dropped out of the literary scene after a very successful publishing run in the 1930s, but before her death her greatness had been restored. In her novels and short stories, she surveyed the internal states of loneliness and victimization with economical fluency and ironic beauty. The most beguiling aspect of her work is that, while a tone of ennui rises from them (as if Rhys couldn't help interjecting a blase attitude about writing them), each word, each phrase, each sentence, on second glance, has obviously been chosen with care to deliver the exact mood of distractedness and dejection. "Mannequin," a tale of luscious brevity, concerns a young woman newly hired on as a model at the salon of a Paris couturiere.

Rhys, Jean. *The Collected Stories.* 403p. Norton, $19.95 (0-393-02375-3).

SAKI
Scottish. 1870–1916.

Want a good laugh? Not just crack a smile, but let loose with a real out-loud laugh? Pick up the incorrigible Saki, pseudonym of Hector Hugh Munro, and turn to "The Stampeding of Lady Bastable," one of the stories in the collection *The Chronicles of Clovis.* In the space of a few pages, the reader delights in Saki's mischievousness, his near-wickedness. A Saki story is short and tight, rendered in a style arch in tone and lacquered with sarcasm. Social pretension and pomposity are the targets of his jabs, and he hilariously deflated such absurd attitudes. Saki's wit could be mean, even grim; but all his stories are pleasurable, if perversely so. Like listening to a friend who is constantly mocking people behind their backs, one reads Saki feeling guilty, conspiratorial— but not about to miss any of the devastatingly funny remarks. Saki's tales are distinguished by beautiful concision: time, place, and character are all conveyed in their essence with minimal elaboration.

Saki. *The Chronicles of Clovis.* 171p. Penguin, paper, $4.95 (0-14-008355-3).

IRWIN SHAW
American. 1913–84.

Shaw's novels—among them, *The Young Lions* (1948) and *Rich Man, Poor Man* (1970)—are perhaps better known than his short stories. But he was prolific in the shorter form, as his *Five Decades* compilation attests; 63 stories are bound within its numerous pages. Shaw wrote stories about contemporary big-city life and about the horrible experiences various people had in World War II—soldiers, victims of fascist persecution. He dealt tenderheartedly with the brutality of life and the narrow interests of people focused only on their own needs, desires, and programs. Shaw's dialogue is sheer delight: snappy, pungent, completely authentic—distinct verbal explosions that go miles toward revealing the truth about the character speaking them. Shaw was careful to understate as he developed a situation, rather than burden the reader with overdone authorial description and commentary. This technique serves to give the stories universal appeal, to raise them above their sectarian settings and circumstances. "The Girls in Their Summer Dresses" is a famous story and justly so. It's an amusing but ultimately sad story about a young married couple's argument, on a Sunday in New York, concerning the man's addiction to watching pretty women.

Shaw, Irwin. *Irwin Shaw Short Stories: Five Decades.* 872p. Dell, paper, $6.95 (0-440-34075-6).

E. Œ. SOMERVILLE and MARTIN ROSS
Anglo-Irish. (Somerville) 1858–1949.
(Ross) 1862–1915.

Edith Somerville and Violet Martin (pseudonymously Martin Ross) were cousins and extremely successful collaborators in writing novels and short stories. Their fiction reflected their roots: the Protestant Ascendancy, the English-descent land-owning class in Ireland, which, at the time Somerville and Ross lived and wrote—the late nineteenth and early twentieth centuries—was on the decline. They wrote a series of comic short stories, originally published in three volumes, about the adventures of one Major Sinclair Yeates, a Resident Magistrate sent from England to the west of Ireland, officially to administer justice. As it turns out, he becomes embroiled time and time again in the chicanery of the native Irish—and emerges as if *he's* the one lacking sophistication. The entire world of Anglo-Irish Protestant overlords and submissive Catholic tenants is evoked with knee-slapping humor—but no meanness. Every story is finely composed with quick pacing and wonderful dialogue, the blarney flying in all directions. The story "Great-Uncle McCarthy" sets the stage and introduces Yeates and other recurring characters.

> Somerville, E. Œ. and Ross, Martin. *The Irish R.M.* 591p. Penguin, paper, $4.95 (0-14-007176-8).

JEAN STAFFORD
American. 1915–79.

While her *Collected Stories* won the 1970 Pulitzer Prize, the late Jean Stafford nevertheless is little recognized outside the narrow circle of avid and quite serious fiction readers and writers. Without a doubt, she should be sampled by anyone interested in the short-story form. Stafford probed squarely into what she perceived as the arid side of life: emotional detachment from people, either self-inflicted or inflicted by others. She wrote often of lonely children easily bruised by adults, or of adults remembering such a childhood. Settings include Colorado, where Stafford grew up, and the places she knew as an adult: New York, Boston, and Europe. Stafford was a lover of big words, long sentences, lots of clauses; she was not one to present an idea head on, but, rather, to circle around it and gradually pry it open to full exposure. "Children Are Bored on Sunday" is a famous tale, and justly so. When Emma encounters social acquaintance Alfred Eisenberg on a Sunday afternoon at the Metropolitan Museum in New York, she is sent into an introspective inquiry into her current state of solitude.

> Stafford, Jean. *The Collected Stories of Jean Stafford.* 463p. Farrar, $17.95 (0-374-12632-1); Dutton, paper, $10.95 (0-525-48101-X).

JOHN STEINBECK
American. 1902–68.

Steinbeck lived in California and wrote of it sympathetically. He is certainly a titan in twentieth-century American literature; but as magnificent as his best novels are, among them, of course, *The Grapes of Wrath,* they should not eclipse his fine short stories. Start with the frequently anthologized "The Chrysanthemums," about a rancher's wife whose low-burning inner flame is renewed one day by an itinerant pot-mender, only to have her heart be broken; or the four-story cycle *The Red Pony*, a moving depiction of the circumstances that thrust a boy on a California ranch headlong into maturity. Steinbeck was always one to focus on the poor and the outcast, on the more elementary levels of social existence as opposed to the more urban and technological. He wrote of men and women taking their lumps in the hard physical and emotional environment of the underprivileged. Steinbeck's style is diverse, but it is essentially a balanced play of directness and studiedness; a sort of raw elegance, then.

    Steinbeck, John. *The Long Valley.* 320p. Penguin, paper, $3.95 (0-14-008038-4).

ROBERT LOUIS STEVENSON
Scottish. 1850–94.

    Stevenson wrote perenially popular novels such as *Kidnapped* and *Treasure Island,* but he was also among the first of the important British story writers. At the top of the list of Stevenson stories is the famous longer tale of dual personality, *Dr. Jekyll and Mr. Hyde.* It demonstrates perfectly Stevenson's propensity for examining moral conflicts in smooth, unobtrusive elegance. His stories roam the globe from his native Scotland to Hawaii, through the centuries back to the Middle Ages. His characters ranged from royalty to poets to sailors. In all of his works, Stevenson offers compelling plot; and, with his superior control in achieving a certain atmospheric effect, he could easily put his reader into just the appropriate mood.

    Stevenson, Robert Louis. *The Strange Case of Dr. Jekyll and Mr. Hyde and Other Stories.* 304p. Penguin, paper, $2.95 (0-14-043117-9).

    Stevenson, Robert Louis. *Weir of Hermiston and Other Stories.* 313p. Penguin, paper, $4.95 (0-14-043138-1).

ELIZABETH TAYLOR
English. 1912–75.

    No, not the movie star. This Elizabeth Taylor was a highly accomplished novelist and short-story writer, held in great esteem by critics and fellow writers. Taylor often probed middle-class suburban life and the gentle men and women who, because of their own little quirks, don't seem to keep exactly on track as they'd like. Jane Austen-like in their sublimity, their sensitivity, and their discreet satire, Taylor's stories are very traditional in structure: beginnings, middles, endings all clearly marked. In the process of producing these conventional compositions, she uses quick but penetrating detail to accent, rather than simply decorate, the story framework. The formal elegance of Taylor's style indicates careful polishing, embellishing rather than impeding the luminosity of her expression. "The Blush" is about a woman entering middle age and having to face the peculiar behavior of her housekeeper; "The Devastating Boys" finds a middle-aged couple taking in two underprivileged London children for two weeks in the country.

Taylor, Elizabeth. *The Blush and Other Stories.* 217p. Penguin, paper, $6.95 (0-14-106157-0).

Taylor, Elizabeth. *The Devastating Boys and Other Stories.* 204p. Penguin, paper, $6.95 (0-14-016106-6).

IVAN TURGENEV
Russian. 1818–83.

Turgenev was a great influence on English and American writers, a seminal figure in the development of the modern short story. His "Sportsman's Sketches" (included in the Penguin edition, *Hunter's Album*) is a series of vignettes published individually between 1847 and 1851 in the Russian journal *The Contemporary* and then in book form in 1852. With poetic intensity, Turgenev captured moments in a nobleman's perambulations through the countryside and, in the process, distilled much of the negative side of nineteenth-century Russian life—namely, the repression of the peasantry (serfdom not being abolished until 1861). With acute irony, Turgenev imbedded a subtle, sympathetic understanding of tyrannized people within lovely descriptions of nature's comforts and surprises.

Turgenev, Ivan. *Sketches from a Hunter's Album.* 267p. Penguin, paper, $3.95 (0-14-044186-7).

MARK TWAIN
American. 1835–1910.

Samuel Langhorne Clemens—Mark Twain—is a permanent fixture in the pantheon of great American fiction writers, noted primarily for his novels *The Adventures of Tom Sawyer* and *The Adventures of Huckleberry Finn.* He is an esteemed humorist, proficient in writing in the colloquial voice of plain river and frontier folk, the practitioner of a shining, clear style. In critical and popular minds, Twain's stories form rather an adjunct to his famous novels. Nonetheless, they are so very stimulating—yarns spun humorously, satirically, and enduringly. There is a delicious personal feel to Twain's tales, as if the author were lounging right beside the reader, chair tipped back, feet up, poking fun of people he's encountered or heard tell of. Among his best short works are "The Man That Corrupted Hadleyburg" and "The Notorious Jumping Frog of Calaveras County."

Twain, Mark. *The Complete Short Stories of Mark Twain.* 679p. Bantam, paper, $4.50 (0-553-21514-4).

EDITH WHARTON
American. 1862–1937.

Wharton was brought up in the narrow world of late-nineteenth-century New York society. It's no surprise, then, that she wrote of that milieu of comfort and power. She was a friend of Henry James and is often referred to as a "disciple" of his, in light of her penchant for elegant investigations of the manners of the well-to-do. But Wharton wrote with more of a serrated edge than what you find in James's smoother, cleaner dissections of social steps and missteps. In other words, she takes *obvious* satiric jabs at social posturing, which sometimes strike the reader as unnecessarily mean-spirited. But Wharton's language is luminously sculpted, and her sense of the short-story form's power-in-concentration is impeccable. "Roman Fever" is a chilling tale—Wharton deftly manipulates the reader then concludes with a literary slap in the face.

Wharton, Edith. *Roman Fever and Other Stories.* 238p. Scribner, paper, $5.95 (0-684-71931-2).

MALACHI WHITAKER
English. 1895–1975.

Malachi Whitaker was the pseudonym of Marjorie Olive Taylor, who reached the heights of story writing in the 1920s and 1930s, then gave up her craft; consequently, her work fell into neglect. It should not be so. Whitaker's work is reminiscent of another great English writer, H. E. Bates, her material keenly drawn from the salt of her native English earth. She writes of good village and country people and their understandable needs and desires. Whitaker doesn't tend to shove the reader right into the middle of things; instead, she provides plenty of warm-up to people and what is going on around them. There is a cool, clear, even flow to her style, a perfect balance struck between hard precision and indulgence in a fondness for the rhythms of lively language. "The Music-Box" tugs at the heartstrings.

Whitaker, Malachi. *The Crystal Fountain and Other Stories.* 176p. Carcanet, paper, $7.95 (0-85635-692-1).

Contemporary Masters

Good—no, masterful—story writing continues into the present day. Experimentation flourishes in Latin America. In Great Britain, where traditions die hard, stories in very traditional veins continue to be written. In Ireland as well. And the world over, generally speaking.

In the United States, the newest trend is minimalism—the writer utilizing extremely spare prose. Plots are minimal—the reader may simply find himself or herself cast into the midst of a dramatic confrontation of some sort. No introduction; no great elaboration of scene and character; just a minimum of development. The reader learns only what is absolutely essential about people and their plights. The sentences that deliver this information are pared down, too. Subject, verb. Subject, verb. Few complex sentence constructions, few modifiers. Very little in the way of embellishment or decoration. A minimalist sentence is sort of like a room done in high tech. The starkness, the very absence of style, *is* the style.

Here is a passage that might be called "antiminimalist":

"His sovereign majesty stood, unnecessary cane in one hand, at the head of the cascade of marble stairs; his haughtiness made his subjects even dizzier as they peered upward to gaze at his superior visage. He began his slow, grand descent, ever so self-important."

A minimalist, if he or she were going to write about a "sovereign majesty"—which he or she probably wouldn't, since ordinary days in ordinary lives seem to go hand in hand with the minimalist approach—but if a minimalist *were* to describe this same scene, he or she might tell it this way:

"The fat king was a buffoon."

What follows is a selective list of the story writers at work today whom I consider the most interesting, the ones most bound to last.

DONALD BARTHELME
American. 1931–

Barthelme is the dean of contemporary U.S. experimental fiction writers. His stories are difficult to grasp and they will infuriate many readers. His sardonic visions of contemporary society bear disjointed narratives—no straight linear progression from point *A* to point *Z*. His stories are akin to puzzles—fragments of dialogue and action and imagery are thrown at the reader, who then must piece them together into a cohesive entity. Political ineptitude, familial and sexual struggles, materialism, the impossibility of language to truly communicate experience: these are the themes of Barthelme's stories. Characters? All kinds of people, the identifiable and the unrecognizable. "The Indian Uprising" is a supreme challenge. This story is either greatly profound, or it may be viewed as simply cleverness disguising an inability to construct a clear plot and easy-to-understand characters.

Barthelme, Donald. *Sixty Short Stories.* 457p. Dutton, paper, $8.95 (0-525-48018-8).

ANN BEATTIE
American. 1947–

Beattie appears regularly in the *New Yorker*. In an assertive, intelligent voice, she probes attitudes and postures taken by persons in love—from the point at which it springs up, to its dying out. Beattie populates her stories with upper-middle-class adults who were brimming with causes in the 1960s, but now, in the 1980s, are only angst-filled. Simple sentences are Beattie's trademark; as a whole, they strike resonant chords. Like brief encounters between individuals in life, her stories are not neatly wrapped up with tidy endings; they are subtle, with a leisurely air but without a hard and fast denouement. "Secrets and Surprises" shows Beattie's skills to good advantage. The young woman narrator, divorced, moves from New York to Connecticut; but it's not a retreat, for life continues to display its inherent round of secrets and surprises.

Beattie, Ann. *Secrets and Surprises.* 320p. Warner, paper, $3.50 (0-446-311140-6).

KAY BOYLE
American. 1903–

Featuring a wide range of settings—reflective of the fact that much of the author's life has been spent abroad—Boyle's stories feature both American and European characters, many of whom have been affected by the hostilities of World War II and its difficult aftermath. These tales are told in traditional narrative form and revolve around value conflicts, either personal ones—who to love, who to hate—or cultural ones between opposing groups: Jewish and Gentile, white and black, different nationalities. Boyle's style is beguiling mix of bluntness and elegant sensuousness. The slices of life offered here are smoothly cut, resulting in subtle but deep character revelations. "The Rest Cure" is a very forceful piece of writing—about an invalid writer. (Reading the dying D. H. Lawrence as the protagonist reveals the story's special poignancy.)

Boyle, Kay. *Fifty Stories.* 648p. Penguin, paper, $7.95 (0-14-005922-9).

HORTENSE CALISHER
American. 1911–

For Calisher, New York is the place to write about; and place is very important in her stories. The environment of, the emptiness of, city life—barren of niceties and warmth—is cast by Calisher as the major limiting factor in derailed relationships. The people she writes about are usually middle and upper class. Calisher portrays New York in sterling language: big words and intricate sentences, all used effectively, stunningly, involvingly. "In Greenwich There Are Many Graveled Walks" is frequently anthologized. It's a tumultuous story of a young man and his domestic travails, friendship woes, romantic possibilities.

Calisher, Hortense. *The Collected Stories of Hortense Calisher.* 502p. Arbor, paper, $9.95 (0-87795-166-7).

RAYMOND CARVER
American. 1938–

Carver is the fountainhead of the minimalist school of short-story writing so currently in vogue. He tells nothing more than what the reader absolutely needs to know about a character or a situation, letting a significant detail here and there denote and connote the present conditions and circumstances. Carver dwells on the commonplace: the small but personally consequential bad turn of fortune in ordinary lower- and middle-class lives. A flat style, forgotten people, a seemingly trivial crisis—these are the ingredients of a Carver tale. "Careful' is a good example of why some people say, "It's not what Carver puts in a story so much as it is what he leaves out"; why some people feel that a Carver story is so wonderfully ambiguous it lends itself to all kinds of meaning and significance; that it resonates with a universal human experience. But this tale also exemplifies why other people think Carver falls flat; an annoyingly simplistic, monotonous tone; characters too boring to care about; not a flash of brilliance in the whole narrative, only a depressing whine, like listening to a tedious next-door neighbor going on about his troubles. You be the judge.

Carver, Raymond. *Cathedral.* 228p. Random, paper, $4.95 (0-394-71281-1).

GABRIEL GARCÍA MÁRQUEZ
Colombian. 1928–

Short stories are not of incidental status in the oeuvre of this winner of the 1982 Nobel Prize for Literature. He is certainly one of the foremost Latin American fiction writers, one of the foremost proponents of that not uncommon feature in Latin American literature: magical realism, a wondrous mixture of realism and truth-stretching, with humor the glue that holds the two together. Often set in the fictitious Colombian town of Macondo, his stories deal with plain village folk, their goals and frustrations, laced with a handful of fantasy that usually takes the form of a physically impossible event. For instance, the ironic tale, "The Handsomest Drowned Man in the World," concerns a dead man, a total stranger, who washes up onto the beach one day. Villagers find him and are awestruck. How's this for hyperbole? "When they laid him on the floor they said he'd been taller than all other men because there was barely enough room for him in the house, but they thought that maybe the ability to keep on growing after death was part of the nature of certain drowned men." Or this: "They thought that if that magnificent man had lived in the village, his house would have had the widest doors, the highest ceiling, and the strongest floor, his bedstead would have been made from a midship frame held together by iron bolts, and his wife would have been the happiest woman." García Márquez's style is both broad-shouldered and lovely, an irresistible combination.

> García Márquez, Gabriel. *Collected Stories.* 320p. Harper, paper, $6.95 (0-06-091306-1).

MAURICE GEE
New Zealander. 1931–

All the stories in the twenty-year, thirteen-story sweep through Gee's writing career demonstrate perfectly his genial, relaxed storytelling voice. Written with a wonderful sense of spontaneity, his tales concern the working out of domestic and social predicaments, with characters generally lying in the border regions between the ordinary and the eccentric. The texture of middle-class New Zealand life is offered in Gee's stories, yet not one suffers from any "local color" limitations. As Gee deftly explores it, the theme of humans facing the foibles of others—within such contexts as youth versus middle age, people finding themselves distanced from other people—is limitless in its appeal. "Eleventh Holiday," a major tale by any standard, concerns a group of couples who, for the past decade, have taken their vacations together. But the eleventh holiday ends differently than the ones before.

> Gee, Maurice. *Collected Stories.* 226p. Penguin, paper, $6.95 (0-14-008804-0).

NADINE GORDIMER
South African. 1923–

She writes of ordinary themes: love, family, the need for security. But Africa, Africa, *Africa* imbues her writing totally—its vast beauty, its difficult white-black heritage. Gordimer is equally at home creating female and male characters who represent all types found in South African society: from whites in urban centers sensitive to the irony of being a ruling minority, to blacks in townships, to residents of Indian heritage. She practices poised diction, but underneath is a searing commitment to humanity. Her sentences are surface-placid but nonetheless bespeak the racial trouble in her homeland and her passionate intention to see a resolution to the conflict. But Gordimer's stories are not didactic; she does not preach politics. Instead she hears hearts breaking when skulls are cracked by repression. "The Chip of Glass Ruby" is a fine example of her social realism, intelligently and straightforwardly rendered.

> Gordimer, Nadine. *Selected Stories.* 448p. Penguin, paper, $6.95 (0-14-006737-X).

GRAHAM GREENE
English. 1904–

The highly respected, avidly read English novelist has written superb short stories throughout his long career. An ardent traveler, Greene sets stories in all kinds of faraway places, from Africa to Mexico. Like his work in the longer form, his stories deal, essentially, with the darker sides of religion and love, but leavened with humor and compassion. There is not an extraneous utterance, description, or incident in Greene's taut narratives. His characters range widely through quirky sorts of people—each one wonderfully involving, clearly defined, well shaded, completely original. "The Basement Room" is one of his most remarkable works. When a little boy is left home in London in the care of the family butler and the housekeeper, his life is traumatized forever. It was filmed in 1948 as *The Fallen Idol.*

> Greene, Graham. *Collected Short Stories.* 367p. Penguin, paper, $7.95 (0-14-008070-8).

AIDAN HIGGINS
Irish. 1927–

A Higgins story wears metaphors stacked up one right after the other, sentence after sentence, without a lot of breathing space in between for the reader to catch up. Each Higgins story shows unusual but vivid word choice: big, strong, unpredictable words that cause the reader to travel slowly down the line of a sentence. Devoid of strong narrative structure, Higgins's works are pieces of character sketch interspersed with moments of rumination on the underside of life. His settings range from Ireland to England to Germany to South Africa; and he uses his pen to shine a steady beam of illumination on the dreariness of minds darkened by loneliness or bent on unfortunate choices in life and love. "Killachter Meadow" concerns the old Anglo-Irish aristocracy that used to run Ireland, and the barrenness of the lives of the four sisters in the last generation of one of those families. Dreary, yes—but arresting, too. The character analysis and verbal dexterity is amazing.

> Higgins, Aidan. *Asylum and Other Stories.* 191p. Riverrun Press, paper, $5.95 (0-7145-0230-8).

MARY LAVIN
Irish. 1912–

Though born in Massachusetts, Lavin has lived in Ireland since childhood; she is considered, ultimately, an Irish, not American, author. But she is acclaimed on both sides of the Atlantic as one of the premier living short-story writers. Love and loneliness within family contexts are common Lavin themes, developed within realistic, often grim depictions of people not getting along or not doing what they really want to be doing. Her stories are character studies, first and foremost. Lavin, drawing on her sense of real experience, dexterously opens a small fissure in a person's makeup and lets the whole character be seen beneath. Though she has a careful, polished, at times poetically intense style, Lavin consciously writes as if her stories weren't to be taken as formal pieces but were meant to be read aloud in a casual setting. "The Long Ago" is a gem; "The Becker Wives" shows her power in the novella-length short story.

> Lavin, Mary. *Selected Stories.* 272p. Penguin, paper, $5.95 (0-14-005602-5).

DORIS LESSING
Rhodesian. 1919–

In Lessing's "The Day Stalin Died," a female Communist writer finds herself distracted by family interruptions and her self-doubt about her true affiliation to the Party. This one story offers a good example of the intense social and political consciousness Lessing brings to her work. Her socialist leanings show through, as do her concerns for racial and feminist struggles. Settings are Africa and Britain, two familiar personal environments. Characters are mixed—all sorts of people. Lessing is unjubilant in her acute dissections of psychology; she's cerebral, a cool analyzer of the more depressing attitudes found in the heart and mind. Lessing's stories challenge her readers to become more alert to the political ways of people.

> Lessing, Doris. *Stories.* 626p. Knopf, $17.50 (0-394-50009-1); Random, paper, $10.95 (0-394-74249-4).

JOHN MC GAHERN
Irish. 1934–

McGahern's stories show his keen sensitivity to the abrupt differences between Ireland's recent past and its present: the difficult transition from rural society to industrial. His stories are built on those particular sociocultural foundations of the past—English domination and the country-versus-city conflict—that bear most heavily on Ireland's future. McGahern deals with the kind of people one encounters every day—outwardly ordinary men and women who possess subtleties that, below the surface, mark them as unique in their own way. The exteriors of these stories are quiet and low-key, but their psychological fathomings reach deep waters. Dialogue in most cases carries the plot; people reveal themselves through what they say. McGahern's lyricism is limpid; while he respects economy, he doesn't make the reader trip over brittle brevity.

McGahern, John. *High Ground*. 156p. Viking, $15.95 (0-670-81181-5).

MICHAEL MC LAVERTY
Irish. 1907–

McLaverty sets his extremely fine stories in Northern Ireland, among rural folk and city people. Their lives are hard, and he renders them realistically: their struggles with emotions toward others, their struggles with the inexorable alterations and adjustments that the passage of time brings. Nevertheless, a gentle tone pervades all his writing. McLaverty is a precise stylist, always stating his words with economy. He allows one carefully composed sentence to evoke a whole string of significance in both action and emotion. His stories are open-ended, featuring a beguilingly demure reluctance to draw the final conclusion—as if he were saying to the reader, "You do it, because I've already shown you what it will be." "The Schooner" is a poignant tale about a young boy's attachment to a model schooner while he's on summer vacation.

McLaverty, Michael. *The Road to the Shore and Other Stories*. 153p. Poolberg Press Ltd., Knocksedan House, Swords, Co. Dublin, Ireland, paper, IR£2.50 (0-905169-56-5).

JAMES ALAN MC PHERSON
American. 1943–

McPherson is young, his output not vast. But his two story collections show a fully mature, stunning writer. His stories deal with contemporary black life in the U.S., on all socioeconomic levels: blacks alienated from whites as they encounter each other in the work place or even in bed; or blacks alienated from each other because their racial expressions take different tacks. A case in point is the story "The Faithful." John Butler, barber and preacher, is failing at both, unable to get with the times and give people what they want in haircuts or in sermons. McPherson's scrutiny of black lives is stringently realistic but warmed by humor and compassion. He writes in a style of elegant rawness, of precise spontaneity.

> McPherson, James Alan. *Elbow Room.* 286p. Fawcett, paper, $2.50 (0-449-24135-1).

> McPherson, James Alan. *Hue and Cry.* 256p. Fawcett, paper, $2.25 (0-449-24192-0).

R. K. NARAYAN
Indian. 1906–

Narayan's stories are microcosms of village life in contemporary India: within broad social contexts—the rigidity of class lines, the consummate interest village people have in each other's business; and on strictly personal levels—individuals' confrontations with the raw deals life hands them and how they cope. His stories are populated with a range of characters, from holy men to astrologers to children. Narayan relies heavily on plot, but his plots are compressed to a few pages—so that the very process of the story's compactness sends off sparks of pungency. Narayan's humorous tales are written in a simple, naive tone—fablelike, as if at the end a moral will be pointed out. "A Horse and Two Goats" details a funny encounter between a goatherd and an American tourist. A memorable piece.

> Narayan, R. K. *Under the Banyan Tree.* 192p. Penguin, paper, $6.95 (0-14-008012-0).

JOYCE CAROL OATES
American. 1938–

Admirably or maddeningly prolific—depending on one's point of view—Oates is undeniably not a consistent writer. In her short stories, especially, she can write a dead sentence and create a tired plot; or she can write a lyrical sentence and create a bouyant plot. She can string a story out to flabbiness or make it perfectly taut. As is the case with several fiction writers past and present, Oates gives her sensibility sharper expression in the short-story form than in her novels. Violence and sexual tension are typical Oates themes; people often frustrated by the latter leading to the former; people alienated from their environment. Her stories are set anywhere—urban, suburban, rural—and she is a master of dialogue. "Where Are You Going, Where Have You Been?" presents the essence of Oates the story writer. Connie is an ordinary, dreamy teenage girl. To her door one day comes Arnold, hardly the knight-in-shining armor she'd been expecting.

Oates, Joyce Carol. *Where Are You Going, Where Have You Been? Stories of Young America.* 352p. Fawcett, paper, $1.75 (0-449-30795-6).

EDNA O'BRIEN
Irish. 1930–

O'Brien writes about her native land and London (her residence for several years) and primarily about love, sex, and women: their romantic needs, their sexual natures, their conflicts with men. But there is nothing sentimental or cloying in her work. Her style is lean but full of kinetic energy, her stories consistently gritty, both emotionally and sensually. A lot of pain and hurt is involved in an O'Brien story. "The Creature" concerns an unfortunate woman in a town in the West of Ireland whom everyone refers to as "The Creature."

O'Brien, Edna. *A Fanatic Heart: Selected Stories of Edna O'Brien.* 461p. Farrar, $17.95 (0-374-15342-6); NAL, paper, $7.95 (0-452-25752-20).

GRACE PALEY
American. 1922–

Paley has written very little, but her critical reputation is high. She is a lean writer, avidly avoiding excessive description. She writes little sarcastic social dramas/comedies set in New York, mostly about vulnerable women—divorced or separated, yet still needing and depending on men. Dialogue, without quotation marks, carries her work and very little happens outside of what people say to each other. Paley's ability to reproduce vocal inflections on the printed page is uncanny. "Wants" is a good story to begin with: four pages, first-person narrator. A woman encounters her ex-husband one day. Then she ponders the passage of time. Despite its brevity, a thought-provoking piece.

Paley, Grace. *Enormous Changes at the Last Minute.* 198p. Farrar, paper, $6.95 (0-374-51524-7).

JAMES PLUNKETT
Irish. 1920–

"The Half-Crown" is an absolutely endearing story, poignant without being precious. It concerns a young man in Dublin—where Plunkett sets his stories—who is in desperate need of some money to entertain a girl he's sweet on. But when a half-crown comes into his possession illicitly, he has a change of heart on spending it the way he had intended. Like many Irish story writers, Plunkett sorts through contemporary life and finds intellectual and experiential narrowness. His stories reflect the economic and social frustration of his native land, as felt by men and women not blessed with birthright or money. There is intelligent sentiment at play in a Plunkett story—he quietly appreciates the short distance between heart and mind in the cause of motivation.

Plunkett, James. *Collected Short Stories.* 299p. Poolberg Press Ltd., Knocksedan House, Swords, Co. Dublin, Ireland, paper, IR£2.50 (0-905169-10-7).

V. S. PRITCHETT
English. 1900–

Not a few critics and well-read general readers claim Pritchett is the best contemporary English short-story writer. In the second volume of his classic autobiography, *Midnight Oil,* Pritchett states that the short story's concise form "concentrates an impulse that is essentially poetic." Every story he writes shows the beauty of this poetic impulse. With rich subtlety, Pritchett observes moments in ordinary experience—in lives of typical working and middle-class types—and finds the idiosyncrasies that, on one hand, make characters unique, but, on the other, indicate a universality in human frailties. Pritchett has a marvelous sense of comedy, leavened with compassion. "The Saint," both typical and outstanding, probes a teenage boy's loss of faith.

Pritchett, V. S. *Collected Stories.* 544p. Random, paper, $8.95 (0-394-71724-4).

ISAAC BASHEVIS SINGER
Polish-born, naturalized American. 1904–

Singer has an expansive personality, and it shows in his stories, as if each one of them were saying to readers, "Come join me in the fun of storytelling." With an appreciative sense of the wonders of human nature, Singer writes about the power and wonder of love and sex despite the hardships life may deliver. His stories are imbedded in Jewish-Polish folklore; set in the Polish historical past (nineteenth and early-twentieth-century shtetls) and in New York City; and limn the lives of religious people, simple people, old folks, writers, tradespeople. Singer writes his stories first in Yiddish, then translates them into English; but Yiddish speech patterns and rhythms remain, leaving his fablelike voice. Singer's works often involve the supernatural or simply fantastic, though realistically conveyed, situations. Take, for instance, "Yentl the Yeshiva Boy," the basis of Barbra Streisand's 1983 movie, *Yentl.* In it, a young woman in late-nineteenth-century Poland poses as a boy so she can go to Yeshiva school and study the Torah and Talmud. Its simple charm assures the reader that such a far-fetched situation is not beyond credence.

Singer, Isaac Bashevis. *The Collected Stories of Isaac Bashevis Singer.* 610p. Farrar, $19.95 (0-374-12631-3); paper, $10.95 (0-374-12631-3).

PETER TAYLOR
American. 1917–

Despite his lack of popular following, Taylor commands high critical respect for his short stories. Taylor writes of his native region, the southern United States—Tennessee, to be specific—in a cool, unflustered style that takes the reader, without confusion or hesitation, through the stories' perambulations. Taylor's work stands poised between gentle sarcasm and an elegiac tone in its depictions of the southern gentility of a bygone age poised against the new values of the modern industrial South. His characters are ruling class: professional people, old landed families, politicians. His stories' abiding hospitality, their sensitive but unsentimental comprehension of the nature of relationships—between lovers, between parent and child, and between races—give them an enduring beauty. "Dean of Men," "Miss Leonora When Last Seen," "What You Hear from 'em?" make up a short list of his most widely appreciated tales.

Taylor, Peter. *The Collected Stories of Peter Taylor.* 535p. Farrar, paper, $10.95 (0-374-51542-5).

WILLIAM TREVOR
Irish. 1928–

Trevor is one of the finest story writers in the English language today. His stories, set in his native Ireland or in England (his place of residence these days), are very traditional narratives with well-marked beginnings and endings and all stops in between. He relishes the significant detail, which, in accumulation, like brickwork, builds a strong edifice. Trevor adeptly dissects the psychology of the strange, eccentric character, from diverse social strata, from child to elder, from shopkeeper to landed gentle folk. He writes in a tragicomic vein with no fancy footwork, only honest pursuit of the truth, love and its rewards and pains, and the frustrations in life that people keep hidden. "Going Home" is vintage Trevor: about a teenage schoolboy and his teacher riding the same train as they go home on break.

Trevor, William. *The Stories of William Trevor.* 799p. Penguin, paper, $8.95 (0-14-006092-8).

JOHN UPDIKE
American. 1932–

The landscape of marriage, particularly the fault lines along which stress and, eventually, cracks will occur, is what Updike explores best in his fiction. That he is an even finer story writer than novelist may become, at some point in the future, the standard critical opinion. Updike's propensity to meander and lecture, readily observable in his novels (though stimulating in its own way), is constrained by the space limitations of the short story; consequently, his brilliance as a writer is expressed in its purest form. The true essence of what lies in the hearts of people is in immaculate focus here. Updike's style also shines in his stories: the careful rhythm of his syntax and his thoughtful choice of high-impact but smoothly flowing images all add up to beautiful sentences. The sequence called *Too Far to Go: The Maples Stories* tracks, unforgettably, the decline of a suburban middle-class marriage.

> Updike, John. *Too Far to Go.* 252p. Fawcett, paper, $2.75 (0-449-20016-7).

EUDORA WELTY
American. 1909–

By virtue of her age, and combined with the highest of critical esteem and widespread fondness among the reading public, Welty, the grande dame of American fiction writers, is frequently proclaimed the best living American short-story writer. The power of her intelligence partnered with the charm of her idiosyncratic, off-beat, or untrammeled characters is an unbeatable match. A Welty sentence is metaphorically profound and syntactically exacting, thus usually requiring a slow pace. Welty writes of rural and small-town Mississippi, of lower- and middle-class whites and of blacks. Loneliness is one of the pervasive themes found in her stories; others include love and what a sense of community brings to an individual. Her stories are often comedies, often fantasies, often modern retellings or interpretations of old classical myths. Her dialogue is rich and unerring in its control of the vernacular. Like two other southern female authors, Flannery O'Connor and Carson McCullers, Welty also writes of grotesques: people on the other side of total social acceptability due to physical, mental, or behavioral detriments. She is, however, able to distill the veracity of her characters' existence more deeply than her fellow writers. "Why I Live at the P.O." is a favorite of many readers. It's a hilarious story about why Sister, the narrator, decided to go live at the post office, where she works, when her sister returns home.

> Welty, Eudora. *The Collected Stories of Eudora Welty.* 622p. Harcourt, $22.95 (0-15-118994-3); paper, $10.95 (0-15-618921-6).

Genre Stories

The telling of supernatural tales has undoubtedly been around as long as the telling of *any* tales has been around. Aren't we all fascinated by apparitions, by what the conjuring of ghosts tells us about our psychology—particularly our fears, perhaps even our sexuality? It is natural, then, for writers who love the short story to turn often to writing ghost stories. Just as mystery novelists turn to writing short pieces of mystery and science fiction authors to little depictions of tomorrow. For within the confines of the short story, effect is heightened; and, in genre literature, effect is paramount.

What follows is, again, a selective list of writers who used the short story form to great effect within the parameters of their particular genre: mystery and detection, science fiction, and ghost stories. More than offering just light reading or simple entertainment, these authors adhered to good story-writing practices.

Mystery and Detection

G. K. CHESTERTON
English. 1874–1936.

Chesterton wrote many short stories featuring a wonderful amateur sleuth: a short, squat Catholic priest, Father Brown. Each and every Father Brown tale is a tightly written package: a murder that the gentle, intuitive priest solves not with hard-core evidence but by ingenious perception based on a point of behavior by the malefactor that escapes everyone else's notice (but seems perfectly obvious once Father Brown has identified it). Written in an exuberantly embellished style, these stories are simply great fun. "The Queer Feet," "The Eye of Apollo," and "The Man in the Passage" are all superior Father Brown.

Chesterton, G. K. *The Penguin Complete Father Brown.* 718p. Penguin, paper, $8.95 (0-14-005977-6).

ARTHUR CONAN DOYLE
Scottish. 1859–1930.

What can you say? Isn't Doyle's creation, Sherlock Holmes, the consummate sleuth, one of the best-known literary characters ever? The list of the best Holmes short stories would have to include "The Speckled Band," "A Scandal in Bohemia," and "The Blue Carbuncle." In each story, the Baker Street detective, with Dr. Watson in tow, applies his famous deductive reasoning to solving mysteries, marshaling the telling evidence that indicates the truth of the matter. Doyle upholstered his stories in richly textured, late Victorian ambience, his characterizations deft, his plots totally involving.

Doyle, Arthur Conan. *The Complete Novels and Stories.* 2v. v.1: 924p. Bantam, paper, $4.95 (0-553-21241-9); v.2: 662p. $4.95 (0-553-21342-7).

DASHIELL HAMMETT
American. 1894–1961.

Author of classic detective novels, Hammett wrote crime short stories for monthly pulp magazines. They have the same hard-boiled style, the same lean-yet-resonant language, as his longer works. These stories, featuring a first-person narrator called the Continental Op, a detective for the Continental Agency, effectively limn the criminal world: its violent furnishings are evoked trenchantly. Plots are well woven; and sharp, accurate street dialogue is a Hammett trademark. He focused on people driven by baser instincts: greed, lust. "The House in Turk Street," with its wonderful twists of deception, is an exemplary Continental Op tale.

Hammett, Dashiell. *The Continental Op.* 319p. Random, paper, $3.95 (0-394-72013-X).

DOROTHY L. SAYERS
English. 1893–1957.

Sayers has become rather a cult figure among mystery aficio-
nados for her incomparable creation, the aristocratic amateur sleuth,
Lord Peter Wimsey. Those who have great fondness for Lord Peter, but
nevertheless find Sayers' novels a touch long-winded, will take great delight in the Lord Peter short stories. Here the reader finds the same de-
lectable comedy-of-manners tone, the same attention to water-tight
plotting. However, the pace is faster, the details less cumbersome to
juggle. "The Entertaining Episode of the Article in Question" is perfect,
vintage Wimsey.

Sayers, Dorothy L. *Lord Peter: A Collection of All the Lord Peter
Wimsey Stories.* 487p. Harper, paper, $8.95 (0-06-091380-0).

Science Fiction

J. G. BALLARD
English. 1930–

Ballard's visions of tomorrow, imbued with both intelligence
and grace, are considerations of *humans* in the future, not aliens with
funny ears. His stories ponder the extension of today's social problems,
such as overpopulation and increased reliance on technology. "The
Drowned Giant" is a sad tale. A giant human washes ashore; his body is
callously regarded, casually defiled. In "The Garden of Time," a fairy
tale almost, certain flowers in a count's garden are what keep uncivil-
ized hordes away from his door. Both stories show sensitivity and origi-
nality.

Ballard, J. G. *The Best Short Stories of J. G. Ballard.* 356p.
Washington Square, paper, $4.95 (0-671-61451-7).

ARTHUR C. CLARKE
English. 1917–

Clarke is a major contemporary science-fiction writer. His moving, disturbing short story "The Sentinel" was the basis of Stanley Ku-
brick's movie *2001: A Space Odyssey.* Written in a pert style, all his
stories are human-oriented rather than technology-oriented, with attention paid to soul, spirit, and psychology. There is artistry in the exe-

cution of these tales—a concern for the well-shaped story with sound development. Devoid of scientific jargon and made-up facts and names to flaunt cleverness or erudition, they are not gimmicky pieces. "The Star" is a classic in the genre. It's an elegant story about the destruction of a highly civilized race due to the explosion of their sun, and what this means in theological terms, i.e., the existence of a supreme being. Clarke's science-fiction detective story, "Trouble with Time," is great fun.

> Clarke, Arthur C. *The Nine Billion Names of God.* 253p. NAL, paper, $3.50 (0-451-14755-3).

URSULA K. LE GUIN
American. 1929–

With a deft turn of phrase, though not a brilliant style, LeGuin fashions highly imaginative short stories combining fantasy and historical fiction. She writes of imaginary countries and cultures in past and present Earth, of their history, politics, and society. She also writes science-fiction stories about new technology and new planets. LeGuin's characters are always well drawn, enticing both in their singularity as people and in how their encounters with adversity are made relevant to our own lives. LeGuin completely understands technical, historical, and cultural elements of the past; and those of the future are realized through her keen imagination. The entire *Orsinian Tales* cycle of eleven stories should be read in order, from start to finish.

> LeGuin, Ursula K. *Orsinian Tales.* 192p. Harper, paper, $6.95 (0-06-091433-5).

Ghost

HENRY JAMES
American-born, naturalized British. 1843–1916.

All of the information for Henry James in the "Past Masters" section applies to his ghost stories, particularly the famous—perhaps *the* consummate ghost story ever—"The Turn of the Screw." When a new governess arrives at an English country house to take charge of two children, she perceives ghostly presences about the place. She decides she must protect the children from the apparitions she is certain they are seeing also. For decades and decades readers and critics have debated a central question about this tale: Are there truly corruptive ghosts present or do we simply have a case of a governess suffering neurotic hallucinations? Either way, "The Turn of the Screw" compels, conveying a most sophisticated chill.

James, Henry. *The Turn of the Screw and Other Stories.* 222p. Penguin, paper, $1.95 (0-14-003026-3).

M. R. JAMES
English. 1862–1936.

This James was a scholar and antiquary, and knowledge of college life and antiquity imbues his ghost stories. His characters are usually learned types, intellectually curious and high-toned when they speak. James is an expert at engendering fear in his readers. Unlike "The Turn of the Screw" by the previous James, there is nothing ambiguous about these ghost stories. His apparitions are unmistakably just that—obvious and awful. Supremely elegant writing, horrible bumpings in the night: just right for scaring the dickens out of any reader. "The Mezzotint" is perfectly creepy.

James, M. R. *The Penguin Complete Ghost Stories.* 362p. Penguin, paper, $6.95 (0-14-009017-7).

EDITH WHARTON
American. 1862–1937.

Refer to Wharton's entry in the "Past Masters" section. Her ghost stories are just as elegant, just as luminous and powerful in their investigation into the supernatural as her tales of manners. "The Eyes," "Kerfol," "Mr. Jones," and "Pomegranate Seed" are among her best.

Wharton, Edith. *The Ghost Stories of Edith Wharton.* 276p. Scribner, paper, $9.95 (0-684-18382-X).

Anthologies

Anthologies of short stories are great resources for gaining acquaintance with a variety of writers, for discovering whose work doesn't move you particularly and whose demands further investigation. The two recent anthologies listed here are outstanding, featuring the works of many writers I've not discussed.

The Art of the Tale: An International Anthology of Short Stories, 1945–85. Ed. by Daniel Halpern. 799p. Viking, $24.95 (0-670-80592-0).

Halpern, editor of the esteemed literary journal *Antaeus,* has gathered more than eighty examples of stories written since World War II. What makes this anthology so unique is its scope—not only are traditional stories matched with experimental ones, but the geographical range is superb. U.S. and European short-story writers are here, of course, but the Third World is heavily represented as well.

The World of the Short Story: A Twentieth Century Collection. Selected and ed. by Clifton Fadiman. 829p. Houghton, $22.95 (0-395-36805-7).

International in scope, with 16 countries represented, Fadiman's anthology of outstanding twentieth-century short stories reflects his own personal judgments. Some writers usually deemed important in the evolution of the short story—such as Sherwood Anderson (American) and George Moore (Irish)—are omitted in an attempt to emphasize the authors Fadiman feels are most relevant to contemporary readers. Fadiman's introductions to each entry are little gems of critical discernment and eloquence.

Author Index

Brad Hooper is assistant editor of the Books for Adults section of *Booklist,* ALA's review journal for school and public libraries. Hooper has published short stories in *Ascent* and the *Maryland Review* and an article on Elizabeth Bowen's short story "The Happy Autumn Fields" in *Studies in Short Fiction.*